POEMS OF THE KNOWN WORLD

POEMS OF THE KNOWN WORLD

by William Kistler

For Sidney,

who sung and danced
with the Gods,
a friend for all seasons,

T

7/16/95

ARCADE PUBLISHING • NEW YORK

FIRST EDITION

Poems collected here have appeared in the following magazines:
Cover Magazine, "Rite of Spring"
Downtown, "The Futures Trader Remembers the Laboratory"
Mirabella, "At a Crossroads Beyond the City"
New Directions, "Ah Visitors"
Night, "Lioness Seen in a Photo Album"
Nimrod, "Cafe of the Found" and "Face Seen Beside the St. James Marquee"
Pivot, "Seeing My Father Again" and "Afternoon"
Poetry Flash, "Through Which Door" and "After Reading
   Izumi Shikibu's Haiku"
The American Poetry Review, "The City of Ancient Voices"
The New Criterion, "Music from an Evening Sphere"

Library of Congress Cataloging-in-Publication Data
Kistler, Wm. (William)
      Poems of the known world / by William Kistler.   1st ed.
         p.   cm.
      ISBN 1-55970-301-6
      I. Title.
   PS3561.I83P84   1995
   811'.54 dc20

Designed by Carol Haralson

Published in the United States by Arcade Publishing, Inc.
Distributed by Little, Brown and Company

10 9 8 7 6 5 4 3 2 1

PRINTED IN THE UNITED STATES OF AMERICA

WITH LOVE AND APPRECIATION
TO FARAH,
AND FOR SUSAN BROCKMAN,
PAULETTE MILLICHAP,
ANDRA SAMELSON,
ROBERT THURMAN —

EACH OF THEIR VISIONS.

WITH SPECIAL THANKS TO
BOB ADELMAN, ANN AZULAY, MARTIN BARR,
RHODA BARR, CAROL HARALSON, RUTH HARDMAN,
ALEXANDRA O'KARMA, JAMES OTTOWAY,
JEANNETTE AND RICHARD SEAVER
FOR THEIR SUPPORT.

CONTENTS

ACTS OF SIGHT

IN THE CIRCLE OF BLOOD

IN DUSK LIGHT

OFTENTIMES ONE REGARDS LIFE WITH PASSION,
IN ORDER TO SEE ITS MANIFEST FORMS.
Lao Tse

IMAGINE YOU ARE DEAD. AFTER MANY YEARS IN EXILE
YOU ARE PERMITTED TO CAST A SINGLE GLANCE
EARTHWARD. YOU SEE A LAMPPOST AND AN OLD DOG
LIFTING HIS LEG AGAINST IT. YOU ARE SO MOVED
THAT YOU CANNOT KEEP FROM SOBBING.
Paul Klee

A CTS OF S IGHT

AH VISITORS

The door cannot disagree
with the space it leaves
as it opens into the room

nor can the writer regain
the words that move his hand
as they enter into the fixed insignia

and not even the sleeper resist
the changeless face that draws her force
as she turns toward the shape of dream,

the vines, however, go on
extending their separate tendrils
too close to the garden trellis

to wake the hidden shade.
Come forward visitor,
whisper to me wilderness,

I saw the lamp swing
when you led this present
so far into my life.

WAITING

It is hidden, it is like a stage left alone
after faces have gone. Words scatter
on the floor, and in the mirror shadows
of a voice, edges of a gesture. Charged.
Dense. And we shift inward toward dream.

It is the hour when my hand first thought
to trace the cords of your neck and you
first took that thought into your heart.
Now am I bound to the forks which have gone

into your mouth, the spoons without effort
which fed your lips. What waiting. What walls
of hidden sentience. And you came over, drew
up a chair, sat down, waited, and I waited,

in this calm like the evenness of water
and in this extended hall of longing
which opens now without hours, a night
filled too entirely out to speak of itself.

Music from an Evening Sphere

The sun stood, then imperceptibly turned,
moved further away behind the dark
pouring of the river, behind the sonorous
chords of the Palisades, the almost
touchable silence of the marsh and tidal

flats. She also stood and this time sang,
her face uncovered and coming forward
as though it were a room being opened
to light, her two eyes leading inward

like infinite lives lying in parallel.
I understood she might hold each strand
of my racial memory, depth of body
and depth of heart. A seeking deeper
than the waters of the flowing river

rose up within me, sent a whispering
out over the radiance of her presence.
An intercellular waking filled every
point between us. The sun stepped further,

drew her voice off into the approaching
train of night. I went home through streets
which held the last inscriptions of light.
I opened a door. Her face was standing
in the mottled shadows where I entered.

ROOM

In a place jagged with buildings like this,
when streets look upward, turn past the sun,
the sky seems to draw the open bowl of its light
back into itself. Each object freed then
of the insistent syllables of form, presses

its own words out into the approaching
darkness. Chairs depart from acting as arms,
become again the branch and trunk of a tree,
the bed no longer stands as a barge frame
but lifts up hills and meadows of rolling linen.

Bit by bit each thing returns to its origins.
I cross to the window, feel a life of car horns
and bird cries echo from building to building.
Her clothes, the sinuous lines of her body,
blend half-hidden into a deep, fugue-like

layering of shadows. A light breeze enters,
slowly takes us over as we loosen each
latching of each of our buttons. It is now
that the weight of my full form comes forward
into the depth of her many folds, she holds,

releases gradually inward, finds the calm
of unhindered being. She and I, both
shrouded in longing and seeking an intensity
we believe we once knew, neither of us
any longer is specific simply to ourselves

as this sea wash wave of merging becomes
a falling away of all need. If ever
we felt as one we see that we have not yet.
This passing back and forth, one into
the other, one around and over the other,

is the single place between us, never
will repeat in this way again. We have
gone out from all others, all else,

are taken hollow by hollow into a breath
which draws the bed, its frame, each last,
thin edge of evening into its passage.

LIONESS SEEN IN A PHOTO ALBUM

The self-certain voices of friends and other
well-informed citizens are rising from the terrace
and going out in loud descriptions of the hunt
as I bend to lift the photographic album up
from off the polished coffee table. Fading there
into the grey and white shadows of the page,
she blends into a thicket of thorn trees,
her eyes worn shut from the weight of the sport
hunter's search. Once she was alive on the plain,

her teeth found the weak among the zebra
and antelope. Her hunger chose the organs
of the heart, the liver. Her sleep finished
in strength. Now mange invades and burns,
and blind, white maggots curl in her droppings.
The animals to whom she was born, whose old,
whose weak she cut down, whose changes, calvings,
migrations, she held in the print of her brain,
all have thinned in the burnished lenses

of telescopic sights. And even in the furthest
cleft of rock, at the most secret water,
in the still thickest hedge, they follow where
she coughs and limps, closes her eyes, stops,
stretches down. For them it does not matter.
They have not fought in the field. They have not
shared with others. They do not believe
in themselves. They kill from across the plain
of long distances. Their hunger stands instant.

THE CITY OF ANCIENT VOICES

It was in the vault of the largest bank
that I heard them speaking in their tongues
of two hundred thousand years, saying, step
into grass, step through the tangled roots
and arms of wildflowers congregating under trees
of dark limbs leafing, through the blood-path
lines of streams carrying the transparent rain-
exhalation of the mountains down from stone
peaks into gorges which themselves are deep
in the form of the calling of the planet heavens.

They were speaking in the vault of the city
and I was seeing the lost, departed birds,
the faces of the painted hunters moving
without breath, the quick as a spark strike
of the cats and snakes which ate the birds,
the forkings of the trees which held the colors
of the birds, the brown caterpillars inching
along brown bark and pulling green leaves
into their white insides before they gave
themselves to the hunger of the birds. And now

we are speaking in the divisions of language
and trying to save ourselves from the economic
order of those who present their interests
in the form of mathematical constructions
standing upon burnished stages of statistics.
I step from the buried light of the vault
into the pooled light of his room. Did you come
to return, he asks. Belief is fading, I say,
I've seen too much of loss. You don't believe
in any of it any more, he says. Do you understand

the breaking of neighborhoods, the demands
of profit, I ask. I understand family,
the needs of my friends. Perhaps, I say, you want
your face to be among and dominate the rolling
faces of television. Perhaps, he says, you want
to end in Brooklyn. I want, I insist, to build
buildings with people who have never had heat.
I am standing, he is standing, we go on
trading barbed notes as still they are speaking
in their tongues of two hundred thousand years,

saying, step into streets, step through turned-over
alleys of broken glass, through tarnished doors
peeling back into boarded windows, through
park grass pressed flat by the metallic weight
of machines, step out of fear and the insistent
bonds of debt, stand in the life of your once-
in-this-lifetime self, receive the star-strewn
field fullness of the heavens, alive beyond beginning
and forming continually as each, every part
bears you on, born as you are, being borne.

POEM OF QUESTIONS

When doubt begins, everything else
is shifted into light, even the letters
I receive printed on pages of paper,
as if each had been sent to me by someone

with a final belief. If I were younger
perhaps I could hold the certainty of their words
fresh in my hands, not begin to wonder
what it was like in the impassioned offices

of those who took up pen, asked me to come
forward, make a witness, they living far off
and having no thought how harsh it is
with the suffering and the wall-like nothingness

which is beyond suffering, of these voices
crowding close in the street, asking for money,
for a room, anything, beside this traveler
who sees he has begun to walk as blind

among the many forms of privilege. And what
has he let himself be taught over the air waves
and through the exploding, gun-shot faces
of television? He has begun to accept

that these lost are not important, he who
at one moment is able to care and at the next
feels the demands of his life pull him apart.
And who is he who frames these lines,

lets them go out like scaffolding into space?
He sees he has become an aging traveler,
one who understands that we have chosen goals
shaped in the forms of our mind's illusions —

limitless wealth, unending temporal life,
rocket-powered journeys to an imagined
edge of the heavens. Such things as take us
far from those standing here. One thing is clear,

the first failure is to give when they are
beside you, then turn without a word, walk on.
Face of the city, mind of the divided,
wealth-driven country, whose citizens fall

out of community as easily as water falls
from the fingers of a shrunken, once vibrant hand,
what are the terms of this life that we have
shaped, in which mind are we naming ourselves?

ACTS OF SIGHT

Metal wheels grind on metal rails,
the demon of screeching is released.
Now the door slides, I am climbing
the shadowy stairs as the sun falls

in long, bar patterns across my face.
I still have my glasses on, I still
feel the words of the text opening
like the colors of completion within me:

when the forms of science and the forms
of ownership are seen as constructs,
the seeker finds himself entering.
I move one step further: when the forms

of thought are seen simply as thought,
the seeker finds himself free.
My hand takes my glasses down. It is
mysterious, an unseen act of gravity,

how the two swiveled arms fall
inward against the frame, come to rest
with successive clicks. I am new
with glasses. I find myself standing

in the mind of those I have seen
standing in the street, blinking, not
knowing whether this sunlight flooding
everywhere around them is a kind

of blindness, whether to fasten their glasses
back, or let themselves go, begin to walk
down through the turning of the street,
see colors, the lined character of faces,

shadows resting in the tireless shade
of doorways, each arrive unframed
like a dawning of notes from a violin
come awake in the folds of the night.

BESIDE THE MUSEUM OF NATURAL HISTORY

A thin rain is falling.

I come up the path under the light,
the first jonquils or daffodils,
I never have known what to call them,
have lifted up their blooms as if they are

gifts held forward by eyes which have been
born again. A few have pushed forward
between the black rods of the fence, bend
their white curves over the pocked surface

of asphalt. On a bench someone is sleeping
under sheets of cardboard. The rain
has begun to soften their shapes in a way
which causes them to fold over the sleeper

like a liquid shroud. What were the words
of the candidate who was perhaps a visionary?
WE ARE GOING TO TAKE BACK THE GOVERNMENT,
OPEN IT TO THE NEEDS OF THE PEOPLE.

He is still waiting for the networks
to let him speak, but they go on airing
unfounded allegations. Such are the actions
of unprincipled men, whether women

would be different we don't yet know.
I step out of the elevator. Here she put
her hand on my back with the lightness
of a spring-tide of hope. In the stairwell

plastic bags full of plastic bottles
are waiting. The bare fire of tungsten light
burns like a voice filled out into anger.
My mother wants to know what to do

with my father's notes about the mechanized
deaths of animals. What is there to say?
What can be done? If you speak they turn
up the volume. If you shout they take you

downtown. Can anyone do anything? History
repeats, they say. What else is there to know?
What can be said? Walk on in. Go to bed.
Plan to begin. Resolve to go beyond beginning.

LINES WRITTEN ON A PARK BENCH

When I was young, with a face untouched
by fear or loss, I wrote poems about death.
They were full of character, wisdom, very
Roman in the clarity of their resignation.

That was before my cells had spoken pain,
decay, the dark hillside of softening bones.
And now I feel I haven't truly lived,
and certainly I haven't understood this which

I have lived, though somewhat more perhaps
than some of these others who go on
telling me I should stop questioning,
embrace the privilege of America, while I

continue to feel I am being pulled through
mirrors of truth and illusion — "the free
market", "free trade" — with my head held
unevenly in my hands, and the misdirection

of those words going on and keeping me
from hearing the broken breathing of people
sleeping on park benches and waking to bend
over trash cans, as cars and guns and the single-

minded, self-assertion of sirens sound
on every corner. How could buildings lined
with marble, and wood from far-distant forests,
hold so much violence? Many are angry

and standing with only weapons in their hands.
Meanwhile share prices continue to rise
and brokers put their money into gold.
It all feels in my open generational memory,

like the last days of the Republic, when
I spoke for the right of small-farm landowners
to sell their crops out of the reach of slave-
produced imports, and the right of the Senate

to legislate such rights. We were defeated.
Farmers were forced into cities, became
dependent on the Emperor's bread. The Empire
lost its base by degrees. But that was

just the beginning of morning. And now
it is still not yet noon. And I continue
to feel I am alone as I speak, and though
there are others who understand, we are

unable to find each other, and no word
comes from the bright gleam of television.
And so I go on trying to reach toward
someone I once held close, in the midst

of loss and violence to find that place
where touch carried the purity of longing
and each might become free of being separate.
Here, in the transparent rising and falling

of these days, which do not flow in any
direction and so hold no form that can be
measured, only divided arbitrarily,
as this poem divides this passage of thought

and every experience connected to it. Here,
time has become the first value and the last,
and is said to be required for understanding
the timeless, filled out, heart's mind

of another. And that time, of course,
is subtracted from wages, which is why
I stopped here, sat down, began to ask
if there might not be a second, somewhere

different life, open in the act of arriving,
open in the halls of departing, traveling
through varied realms, unmeasured, without
owner and going on with each, where

each is felt as friend and fellow oarsman
on the river, and they fold their arms,
fall into sleep, into a dream which now
is walking and as it walks, stops, looks

directly about, its eyes uncovered, its voice
also walking, and full, free of fear.

THE MOMENT IN ITSELF,
THE MOMENT OF ITSELF

Each part of me wants the thing it thinks
it has not got, the woman it has not known,
the place it has not yet been. Where was
the beginning of hunger? Where the dividing

from peace? Was there ever rest from need,
the moment therefore in itself, the moment
of itself? The one, open instant
I do recall, was the sound of two blocks

being struck amidst the even silence
of a rock garden, as if a wall had parted,
left a space between where no sound or light
had ever been, and where the inverted whisper

of you, my continuing other, wanderer's
voice, might call me down unmarked stairs
to a different and longer departure.
The moment in itself? As if there were

a center to the day and to the people we are
talking to, as if we were not at every moment,
shifting, turning over, waking in the expanded
field of the many. The moment of itself?

As if there were a single emotion we were
exactly feeling, precisely reaching toward,
as if there were one truth of person
we were walking with, becoming attached to,

slowly turning back from. And if I take
this moment differently, take myself differently,
let each thing arrive effortlessly toward me,
pass effortlessly from me, am I then free,

able to see each life in the numberless
shapes of its continuing? Or is that hunger,
which I was just held in the fingers of,
the single mind of the modern — to be

in search as if alone, to need to hold
to each thing owned, to need to own more?

At the Edge of the Park
Under Chestnut Trees

We were walking in shadows of chestnut leaves,
each of them broader than the length of her hand.
Departure wrapped itself between us in thin,
web-like lines, very close in strength
to the hunger we had felt when first we began
to know one another. She paused, turned left,

started down toward the bridge at the river
as the leaves came together, shut out the light.
Memory rose up within that moment of darkness
as rich as the deepest center of a forest
grown so full leaf by leaf that each tree limb
might seem freed, released, able to take itself

down into what never was a ground but the sum
of all of our inventions. We were parting,
each meeting and each choice of conversation,

each room and every lost shape of passion
merging like an undercurrent in the wake
of a broad ship, flowing back, gone, not to be
seen again, only the last strands of nostalgia
holding for a time in the frame of what
might have been. The future, too, fell away,

seemed ended. We could not know when either
of us might take up a form of mind, a kind
of violin without strings, watch music begin,
the rising of fugues. There, disguised within
the harmony of many themes, we might step again
toward the act secret in the thought of meeting.

HOTEL INDETERMINATE

It was a pain so broad within me that it felt
like an idea of pain which had entered
and would not leave, a continuous ringing
without a bell, like stones in a stream
with water forever flowing over them and wrapped

in the same grey-blue which finds its color
in the narrowing darkness that comes to us
just before dawn. You can never know
how you will feel when you open a door, find
you are in a room apart from where you thought

you would be, with different feelings taking
different chairs and an unexpected depth
of sadness coming forward to rest upon them.
This is not what one thought would be next,
and now it seems that this shifting present

will always be this advancing wall of pain
with no other life which can even be glimpsed.
If I could sleep I might wake somewhere else,
but now at the edge of sleep I still can feel
her hands closing around each of my arms,

pulling me close to her in that same unresolved,
I want you, I can't accept you, ambivalence
fixed within the moment that we parted.
I am a life seeking the unrestrained
opening of its life. Each day as it begins

seems unalterably smaller. I think I remember
that when wells are empty, rain comes down
out of the torrents of spring to fill them.
Is there such a season? I tell myself
I believe it does still exist. I tell myself
I will get up, I will go out to look.

The Journey Back from Iona Abbey

A small island with low, stone-embossed hills,
an abbey church shaped from those same stones,
a carved Celtic cross standing before it. The sea,
the sheep grazing, the gentle ringing of matin bells
signaling prayer. The feeling that each element
was woven into every other. Peace. I came walking
down the hill just as the green prow of the ferry
was lowered to the slant of white concrete. I held
field flowers, growing at the wall of the abbey, singly
in my mind. A grey mist was passing over everything,
the sun shone through intermittently, illumined
separate trees, stones, like a sudden memory.
I crossed the ferry deck, stepped over a metal frame
into an almost dark room, sat down beside a window.
The abbey drifted back into the mist as if it were
a dream exposed to the light of morning whose shape
is slowly covered with consciousness. Now I saw her
standing to my left, her body parallel to mine.
She was watching me while watching passengers
on the deck. We stayed bound that way, not looking
directly at each other but touching with every sense,
as the sea went on like a completed life, closing over
behind us. I began to read without letting
her presence fall from mine. Women, of course, almost
always choose men, though letting us by appearance
pretend otherwise. I went on reading. In my youth
I would have stepped across that small space,
spoken my name, suggested letters, that we somewhere
later meet. The boat turned. The prow was lowered
to the shore. Passengers began to walk off across it.

Now she crossed in front, between the two
rows of seats, took up a package of cigarettes,
turned, looked into me, a slight, whimsical,
ironic question at her lips. Neither of us moved.
A bond of knowing as before, only deeper,
more complete, passed between us. New passengers
began to enter. Our eyes tightened. I rose,
crossed the length of deck, stepped over onto
concrete, turned as if pulled by a voice as low,
as insistent as my own, looked back at the open
frame of the door, saw only darkness, walked on,
turned again at the top of the concrete, a cigarette
began to glow at the height and in the depth
where she had been, a light drawn deep, flaring,
as though my eyes had touched her at some
remembered center. She came out from the darkness,
stood at the door. The sun shone through, lit
the green prow, the white concrete, an orange-red.
A general fire rose up between us, we were
as apostles of sight, breathing in a language,
surrounded in a passion not yet written. I was on
macadam, still walking backward, my shoes landing
with a softer sound, my eyes bound in a marriage
primordial, a man setting out to cross the hills,
the plains far off, a woman working an inland sea.
Medium height she was, tending toward thin,
blond hair twisted slightly and rusting in the red
sun, eyes encircled with the hunger of freedom,
with the need of feasting at the frameless bed
of experience. I kept walking backward,
turned as the road turned, was alone without
waving, was alone without knowing how I kept
from calling or going back. Kept walking backward.

IN THE CIRCLE OF BLOOD

RITE OF SPRING

Though you are lost to me forever, strike me,
bend down, beat me, though I fling you back,
send out words after you so that
the forest rises up, enters in between,

though you force back every stone before us
and they crack and fall around us,
pull both my arms off and then your own,
throw them against cliffs, still you

belong to me, still you seek me out, young man
hiding in the bushes, young man searching
in the flowers. Forever I do not leave,
forever I remain, yours that I am,

young girl dreaming in the stems of grass,
young woman looking out from the towering trees.

WORDS SPOKEN AT MIDNIGHT

They were not born under the trees,
they came to us through the trees,
with a God whom they said contained
all Gods. We let them come in.

Now the Choctaw are gone and the brown bear,
almost all of the beaver
and the fish from the river that runs
down through the plains of grass.
The grass now is wheat, and the wheat
is standing under layer upon layer
of white ash which they call phosphate.

Where was it that we came from? What
were our names? Though I call three times
none of our brothers, our sisters, return.
Is this a place I have known before?
Even so I will go on speaking, I will
speak until the voices of our fathers,
our forgotten mothers, are heard.

Tonight I will sit in the thundering
of buffalo, tomorrow I will lie
in the turning of eagles, here
in the electric burning of the white dream,
here in the fiery imaginings of taverns,
I will stand and repeat our names.

Black-As-A-Crow's-Wing and Wing-From-The-Sky,
I will repeat their names, Shinnecock
and Shoshone, Kiowa and Lakota,
Face-Of-Many-Seasons and Smile-Behind-The-Eyes,
I will speak their names,
Friend-Of-Deer and Many-Men-Walking-As-One,
Bright-Flower-Beside-The-Stream,
I will speak their names.

I will call out until the waters
run upward, burying the cities, swelling
the oceans, flooding the doorways of machines.
Work will come back into our hands,
the strength that was between us
will come into our arms, we will reclaim
each fallen tree of our lost history.

City Landscape

I stopped at the corner of the park.
The bell-like chiming of brass hand cymbals
rose among the engine bursts of the street.
I turned, a black man seated as an orange-robed

mendicant, finished the striking. His back
was as straight as the bars of the iron fence
standing behind him. I took coins from my pocket,
put them among coins lying on the cloth

before him. He raised his head, smiled
more deeply than I had seen in years of city
meetings. Sadness had gone from his eyes,
they were broader than the shaded face of guile,

all language was held free within them,
each color spoke knowledge, the linking
of many energies brought together
from the thousand sightings of experience.

I made the joined-hand sign of respect,
stepped back, felt myself moved to a different
understanding by the calm of his presence.
The path through the park led under elm trees.

Beyond were the tiled walls of the subway
where people were stepping around pools
of dark urine, and trains were continuously
being pulled forward out of tunnels,

bearing the flame-like calling out of names —
Kronos, Angelito Negro, Fly and The Hittite
Brotherhood. Another world. Fierce seeking
after recognition. Violence spreading

into abandoned places. His eyes bore me
forward. I would be watchful. I saw
these others as travelers like myself,
brought down here without choice, their eyes

holding the hand of fear, holding the hand
of anger, alone without enough of time
or space to waken into peace. I would try
to stand in peace. I did not fear them,

only those driven mad by smoke
from the white powder of the coca plant,
harvested now where once it had grown wild
in the far, river jungles of the Andes.

FACE SEEN BESIDE THE ST. JAMES MARQUEE

Coming from across the river, from beyond
the far-off grinding of trucks leaving the city,
coming toward us from a sun which sends
only life-energy and takes nothing back,
like the hands of one newly in love,
the light crosses through misting rain,

meets the light falling from the letters
of the marquee. They mix in his knotted hair,
in the rain holding to his face which moment
to moment drops from his chin, lands on salt

bagels. Dressed in brown corduroy in summer
he is a mountain man surely and has found
his way here from far off, from a corner
of the Pyrenees, from the Apennines,
from the ancient escarpments of Azerbaijan.
No one is buying bagels in the rain.

He lifts the handles of the cart. The tires
turn so slowly no sound rises from the street.
I see that he is old, weighted with the tribal
knowledge of thousands of years. The lights

switch off then back on. We are all old
beside the comic intent of the music
about to begin. It is late summer,
the time of heat in the Northern Hemisphere
when this city of mixed races stands
and talks more slowly to itself in the hope

of finding a place of mind at peace
before the long-forgotten division of tribes
and the continual searching for food,
before the force of harsh mountain wars
printed on a face newly arrived
from a country none of us has yet seen.

We stand a moment longer. The sun
is covered once again by rain, the lights
of the marquee reflect in the street.
He turns the corner. His cart is small,
quite small, among the trucks rolling forward,
shaking the windows on Eighth Avenue.

THE FUTURES TRADER REMEMBERS
THE LABORATORY

When the price of oil went up, the price
of gold turned, went down, this was called
unprecedented, beyond statistics.

The next month I found myself without rent,
no longer a member, standing up, eating
red beans. Each one looked as familiar

as a friend whom I once had known well.
Each achieved a certain size, I could feel
its weight and what it was about to say.

Something in the look of their shapes
brought to mind my first experiment, the late
afternoon sun striking the rounded sides

of the beakers and flasks, the raw, red,
pinned-down flesh of the frog's legs speaking
directly to me and saying that they did not

exist apart from the watery ponds of earth.
They drew back, laughed, in the way I wish
I could, when I touched each of their nerves

with electric current, then gave them a room
in the scientist's home for the dispossessed,
in the white hotel of the recording chart,

that closet for the known, the predictable,
which I now see I too am standing in.

Across a Broken Landscape

The dead were lying on every side when
I looked into the surface of her eyes, torn
by the wounds of guns, swollen with hunger,
burned white in the craters of ditches.

I saw her breath come in and go out as if
forced from one lung slowly into the other.
Blood coated the gratings of storm sewers,
stained the left-after shell casings.

Each of us walked between the fallen
without knowing if we would end among them.
Belief had left, was burned flat, only broken,
severed hands held the form of existence.

Other lost were walking also. Mysterious,
unsought ribbons of hope joined between us
as we met, as though the radiance of rain
unexpectedly was falling in first leaves.

Slowly her voice, the intricate markings
of her mind, returned. Our lives hung
upon us there, as if they were dry, thin
robes worn past further use. We went on,

whether as living or dead I cannot say,
I do recall that even the shortest step
in that journey slowly hollowed us as one
into the form of an empty offering vessel.

Hour at the End of a War

The sun burns in the depth of background
as it shines into that darker foreground,
a candle stands on the Empire table
where chairs turn in upholstered curves
and shadows widen across the single door.

A motionless house with light as voice
and the whole of the strength and breadth
of legs, of arms, of flesh is spreading.
And where my fingers meet her back, shape
begins. I let them go out, it lengthens.

I let them go on out, it deepens.
BOMBS DROP INSIDE, IN MY MIND,
SPLINTERING TREES, BLOWING UP EARTH.
We step out of practice, we step
out of act, each touch releases, is freed.

When was it, where was it, that we knew
each other? Habit departs, every reaching
after the spent past. A KNIFE, I CAN SEE,
IS SLOWLY TURNING INTO THE STOMACH
OF A PRISONER. I CLOSE MY OWN EYES,

THAT FACE FIXED IN ANGUISH IS SET
ON THE INSIDE. Space remains, and remains
open. The field of sight turns through.
Now begins life lived after this war
we were made a part of. I SEE THAT I HOPED

48

THIS MOMENT WOULD BLOT IT OUT. HIS TORN
FACE IS STILL INSIDE. Desire stands
forward on the columns of our eyes. Light
imperceptibly enters through the veils
of our senses. UNSPEAKABLE SADNESS

EXPANDS AND IS BLACK WITHIN ME, LIKE
SHROUDS OF MOURNING, OPENING, OPENING OUT,
HANGING DOWN. Arrive, and then
arrive together, and finally we have
arrived. Candle and glass and lamp

absorb the moment we now are in,
motionless long lines of sunset pass
from bone to crest of illumined bone.

Near the Burial Ground

She knelt by the river bank to break the purple
flowers at the bottom of their stems, just above
their roots. Soldiers were passing on the road
below, now she could not take them to his grave.
She placed their long iris faces in a hollow
between two tree trunks with their heads up.
She sat. She waited. She pictured the group
of them resting against the grey marker stone.

The past was in the mind anyway, all of it,
what and wherever they had been, each of their
passionate, their intuitive joinings. The blooms
were feminine, of course, so she would have
wanted to bring a leafy branch along, lay it
lengthwise on the ground, a masculine form
to complete the image of their union. But even
that was in the implied order of civilization

and they had stood apart in their deepest hopes,
latter-day naturalists, democratic socialists.
Better to have left the torn flowers rooted
as they were and taken away the gravestone,
then he could give himself over in the full
mystery of the field. Better to have left them
scattered among the grasses and tangled thickets,
left them as lights to the pollen-seeking bees.

She would not come again, or no, she would
yet return, down the hillside of imagination,
into the earth of memory and waking. By that
path he would be there, not smiling likely,
but filled white in the fullness of dream.

SEEING MY FATHER AGAIN

It was April, I was looking into Van Ruisdael's
painting of trees, vines, rotting limbs,
standing and lying in patterns of sunlight,
as my father balanced the box of medicine bottles,

then let it fall as if it were a plumb line
down from the third-floor bannister onto
the entrance hall sofa. It bounced, tilted,
spilled the many colors of its vials and capsules

across the oaken floor. He was not angry,
the struggle against death fell from his face
as if it were an exhausted warrior. He had
never shouted or tried to hold on to anything.

I think of him, now, as the one truly gentle
person I have known. He did not speak but turned,
walked to his bed, the gaunt bones pushing up
frail knobs under the shoulders of pajama linen.

April, again, as I see him lift his arms
among the limbs spread across the painting.
Sun in green, light networks of buds. Sun
as a stream in which they breathe, each one

woven through him in the crystalline linking
of time's substance. Dark limbs lifting upward
and a bird, its throat back, beginning to sing.
Bird black, buds opening, westward sun of time

beside my father waking as each of these words
assumes his face upon a page which slowly
begins to curl, turn itself over, wrap through
his extended, unbridgeable arms of longing.

THE PASSING BY OF A WRITER, THE WALKING IN OF NIGHT

As though trapped within the overexposed
face of an aging photograph, the last grey
light of evening passes down the street, frames
each of them where they join together, take one-
another by the arm, their young voices going up

like the briefest of fireflies into the summer
air, as they whisper secrets and secret words
to their friends and first lovers. I remember
standing in that advancing darkness with just
a thin shadow of light, up the path, in the park

at the top of the hill, free in the knowledge
that they would return across each cycle of seasons
and someone like myself would always record them,
hold their form forward so that they could see
themselves, believe. Free I felt, like the windows

of a tall house, able to look within, observe
myself standing as if in fact, but in truth
transparent, a spirit like a membrane, able
at the same time, to look out into the folding
flow of the street. Such a window knows itself

as poet, does not fear to have its setting
changed, watch the entering in of other voices,
a different generation, new names brushing close,
nudging one another, as night bends all the way
over, motions to itself, walks on through.

EVENING: SAGAPONACK

I am sitting on the cedar boards
which Steve cut. Evening is slowly
passing its masked and mauve blood
through grey veins of night mist. Every

green is turning black, the very light
leaves of the birch are turning from side
to side, as if looking slowly about
before entering an unknown room. Black

birds are coming into the silver-green
olive bushes, their wide wings dissolving
into shadows of limbs. Only their calls
are heard, rising like tendrils of flame

from within their darkened place. The clear,
bright streaming we think of as light,
and the hidden, covered fullness
we understand as being without light,

balance beside each other, as if they are
notes of opposing pitch, blown from the same
flute. There is no other place I seek,
no knowledge here not free to be known.

These presences are subtler than naming.
More and still more darkness waits
to be seen. I will wait to see it.

After Seeing the Lost Lover Wake on Stage

It wasn't as we imagine it is when someone
we hold close has fallen into what seems
a death coma. At the moment she awoke
she recognized him immediately, as if

she were not lying motionless just
above the place where death had spread
its opaque and seamless blanket, but had known
he would be present and he would reach

at once to touch her. In such a waking
all their history would be lost and go from them
like the music of musicians whose instruments
are broken, whose chords must be brought back

bit by bit on the edges of makeshift strings.
If she had been lost in sleep near me
I would have whispered esoteric prayers
into her ear, cast rose hips and herbal essences

about the bed, touched her at the upper end
of the line of her neck, attempted to transmit
the memory of our lost tenderness. Wait.
Sit. Receive no insight. Fall almost

into despair. Search in mind for a means
to bring her back. Realize no medicine
could cure but the faith simply of waiting.
Wait, gradually release each sense

from the mind of waiting. Deliver every energy
into her clouded mind. Wait in a room
that does not change, that remains white
sheets, white walls, wilting flowers. Wait

in a running waterfall of continuous time.
Wait in an open tunnel of commitment without
apparent end. Wait. Stay so long her first
stirring would seem not real, but the figure

of a dream turned into fantasy. Then I would
inhale long and hold, as when a depth of sand
receives its first wash of sea and swells open.
One eyelid might tremble, the other slowly

wake then close, then wake again, and there
would begin an unfolding in which the past
and each intimation of future would join
between us. We both would link in a shared

beam of sight, watch the valley of separation
shrink to one moment beside us, like a hand
alone without an arm, disengaged from search,
able to fall from longing, seeing itself free.

THE CHORDS BETWEEN

We are sitting in the furthest corner, half-
hidden in shadow, eating rice and white beans.
The slow, knotted chords of nocturnes wind
like smoke around us, fill each with blood
from the cell of unspoken understanding.

Notes enter, continue entering and in
the same motion recede like waves which
move always toward the sands of release
then find themselves passing into the air
of their own passage. Our eyes enter

the life of each the other. Both angular
with long noses. She with wide, green irises
set between black, cubist planes of tumbling
hair. Myself with the blue of the heavens
deepening when I look at her. This is

the night we are to decide if we will go on.
Chords open and close around us. She
leans toward me, we join without touching.
What if there were no music, she asks,
would I exist for you like this? I begin

to say there is no moment we can possess
and no life not shaped by circumstance.
The words are to the side of her question,
I go on holding her in the answer of my eyes.

UNDER THE NOON OF LONGING

When I remember that every pattern
between myself and others continues
and goes on until it seems that each
is too fully written into me to speak

of itself, then it calls out loud
how you remain and walk in my mind
like the last orange embers Lautrec left
burning in Jeanne Avril's eyes. He, too,

ate of the night and drank his mornings
in the smoky cave of absinthe. And what
can I know of you, now, my voluptuous,
lost friend? If only there were some

part of the vase of your hip left after,
I would take that curve into my teeth,
swallow. You would be alive in me
as I was in you. We drank without moving.

Filled with blood, we were one in devouring.
Did you take or did I enter? We might
both agree, without speaking, that it was
done together. Though now in this quiet,

lying as thick as my lost hunger, I see
that you came fully into me. And further
than I intended. Down each vein you went,
into each corner, turned back, shadowed

every cell. You did not stop entering.
You were then and you go on as the harshest
virus. The many heads of you look at me,
pull back their laughter, walk beyond my voice.

Light enters, finds no person to illumine,
no lungs, no base of feet, only thought of you
which is airless without your form, which is
a calling for presence, a calling into a river
deeper than the darkest night gorge of memory.

View from the Museum Window

There was such a rage filling the streets
that she looked at me as if I were
the last man. I am dead as well, I said,
how else could I be standing? It was
a question of what one could imagine,

and I saw that in the dialogue between
she and I, we might both bring into mind
a sun arriving through the harsh, orange
colors of the anger surging around us.
I began to wake, I could see branches

held in the light of becoming, where
her hands were being offered like fruit
from the vine of the original universe.
And with a pen lighter than form and dipped
in the grey-brown ink of resignation,

I begin to outline the worn face,
the worn arms, the dust-stiffened pants
of the carpenter in the courtyard beyond
the museum window, where his head
has tilted down in sleep and an apple

sits at rest in the creases of his hand.
I understand I must etch each aspect
of his face, in the midst of flame and conflict
hold firmly to them as he still holds
to the irreversible dignity of work.

Now, in a far back room of the museum, a guard
stops to look at his watch in the motionless
stone presence of the Goddesses of the past.
A male totem calls out – WAR – and bursts
the glass. I imagine the peace of the wash

of her essences flowing over me. The moment
and unending fire of rage and destruction
is covered by the heart's deepest waking.
Here, and in the court, and in the furthest
corners of the fields beyond, each thing

finds its being where the ants are eating
the seeds from the flowers, then fertilizing
other seeds. All of us at once are holding up
a mirror of need to every other and looking
deeply into it — ancient, ageless birth of sight.

IN DUSK LIGHT

BACK OVER THE END OF DAY

Back over the end of day
came the darkness of clouds,
then rain, then sun outlining
them as light, as if a door

had opened fully to reveal
a bare room along whose walls
memories blent like water
and out of the corner of which
the foot of a form was stepping.

From first to last, in day,
in the extended black of night,
there is no holding to the life
already named, still fully known.

NIGHT MARKET, TAIPEI

The rolling sounds of a Chinese pop song
fill the air already filled with lights
from electric pinball games. I, or rather

the mind I presently am, is standing
in a doorway looking onto a street
framed with racks of clothes. People

without money are trying to sell to other
people without money, who themselves
are hesitating and thinking of the falling

apart of such clothes. Fish sellers
are cooking the scraped skins of fish.
Faces foreign to me are eating.

A white dog stops, and in a posture
of listening for his master's voice,
resembles a dog I held in my arms

when I was eight. I am different now
from what I was then, though closer
than I have been since, taken as I am

with wonder at the immeasurable
length of each moment. My mind opens
without restriction, and does not hold

to any form, as the chimpanzee sitting
on the counter in the shop across the street,
steps onto the top of the cash register,

lifts an arm up, begins to swing from a bar
fastened overhead. His owner hardly notices.
He is showing a jacket sewn with four materials.

Is there anyone here I thought was here?
If I did not have money I would have to go
as a grey-haired mendicant among these people.

Who would I be then? I have nothing they need
and not even anything I truly need. And who
am I, and what have I brought to this place,

if not these images of myself? This present
one, the calm, the all-seeing. Those others,
lover, shaper of thought, he who works

into exhaustion. Each takes its form
from the weight of the things surrounding it.
We are not as we believe, free and independent,

people and events are the field which shapes
the steps we think we separately take.
What then does this mind have left to recognize

as itself? Just this rediscovered peace,
this feeling of being able to move
from one moment to the next in openness,

this feeling of release which even now
a breeze is beginning to pass through, to lift
the edges of, to reveal the starry emptiness of,

this freedom which comes forth when I have
traveled far off, seen the limits of this self
which daily clothes itself with habits,

felt the sense of being in receipt of forms
without limit. I enter a room. I am given
a view from a window looking onto a harbor

from which two ships are departing in different
directions. I understand this is a present
which moves neither forward nor back, up

or down, but exists at once with every other
part of this moment which turns and goes on
and speaks as seamless, as sea, as one voice

passing into and filling the place of another.

Cafe of the Found

She leaned across the table to place the spoons
on the other side, this brought her eyes into
contact with mine, this brought both our hungers,

written in the present that is as blue as a sky
on which being is being imprinted, together.
Her shoulders came forward, her back tilted

into round. She was looking at me but she was
with him. His hand moved against the flexed
curve of her hip. Change entered, the unfurling

colors of the unexpected moved across her face,
like a storm which broadens, fills the plains
of an unused countryside. Now she was standing

in the continuous rolling of the unguarded,
this brought the gradual closing of his eyes,
the further opening of mine, as if I were

alone at the gates of a long-forgotten city.
She was standing. He and I were sitting. Each
of us was being washed in the waters of evening.

AFTERNOON

This standing up to walk out, this ending
that will never end, this waiting to go
away from you in order to find again
the freedom of coming back. This going on.

This holding onto a fence and looking not
into the park but into the many branchings
of your face. This pausing to talk to someone
and seeing the dark edges of your smile

looking out from behind their eyes, while
also I know they are picturing someone else,
somewhere else. I walk on. I begin
with the curve of your shoulders and then

I draw all of you into the circle of my arms.
You fade into me, merge and take me with you.
We fall through the open fingers of time,
sit down without concern at your small

table. You put your hands on my face.
We introduce ourselves into a meeting
set beyond expectation, and therefore
beyond fear. You hold my presence to you,

a joining of eyes within a knowledge
we enter without limit. Memory is not there
nor any other life already experienced,
only the blending bit by bit together,

as though light were passing into water,
as though water found itself rising into air.

WAKING IN THE MARRIAGE ROOM

Goodbye to the sun withdrawing out
of these squares and streets, out of
each definition and figure of speech,
leaving us in this room of after-light
where only the memory of flame exists.

Goodbye to the romance of imagination
and the dream-portraits of women too various
ever to be found. Goodbye, nothing more,
to the belief in permanence, solutions,
the syllables of this life open themselves

in lines of change. So I return, find
anger gone and a new blouse surrounding
your neck as a sign of forgetting. Go on
each day as you have, with something
different, I see the wisdom in it now.

Goodbye, finally, to the mind for which
the ideal alone exists, darkness
and the deep of night drink perfection
then remember it in the form of the bowl
on the table at the hour of breakfast.

Goodbye to search, to the pretense of within,
I give myself to the flesh of the world
which bears me forward, the speechless
sighing of the veins of your legs, the subtle
labyrinth of your walls of passage, the first

flags washing along the shelf of your sleep.
I give myself to the life of your presence
which bears me across, its continent
of becoming is effortlessly joined.
Across each imagining time flows,

within each thought days are removed.

The Life Continuing

Now you are leaving. You are going
down a hall into a street I will not see,
into a life which might take any form
except this one that I am present in.

You return. You are without edge, unbroken,
as if you had come in from an endless
beginning. More calm than I remember,
you are gentler than I have yet imagined.

You are before me as the open, drafting
waves of the ocean of the senses, as full
as if in some lost, other time you have been
every pair of eyes ever looked through.

I take your hand to my face which is
the same as my heart. I take your teeth
to my face. They are whiter than your hand,
hard at their ends and washed in the living

breath of the blood. Your eyes come forward,
turn, walk in the shadowed depth of dream
as if it were the illumined shore
of wisdom. I place my mind next to yours,

we enter the first room of the unfinished.

FACE OF MYSELF

These incidents and unbroken occurrences
of fact take me forward from day to day,
there is never a moment which is not a door
closing onto a room, onto a chair, across

a table laden with facts. And when
I have lived through the last of them
there is still this mask which walks on,
remembers itself first as my face.

Each experience in the world of events
is what my identity constructs itself of,
it is what I report of myself and what
I would peel back. I am this history

for everyone else. It goes on, is continuous
and registers every moment into its record.
But if it were an eye that was separate,
if it could imagine and then lead on

to a different place, I would turn, walk in.
You would be there, the breadth of your life
beside mine, the bone surge and the blood
dark in its channeled running. And the farther

I would go out of myself toward you,
the further I would step forward into
this other, open self, alive behind the face,
dreaming behind the mask, finding itself

at the heart of each thing. The shortest path
toward these sites of my many-sided self —
this lamp shedding light on this table,
that tree bringing forth leaves from within

the veins of spring — is out on the lines
of the eye, into each life where I feel
I am already in full. Then step again,
this time beside you. You are there,

turning yourself with the ease of a flower
directly toward morning. The door finally
is open, each of us now is clearly seen,
holding to the forms of our many faces,
every band of beloved sunlight.

Seeing the Chestnuts

As if at once, each point of phenomena
arrives toward me streaming and seems
a presentiment of all future knowledge.
At other times it is slower, each event
opening into the weight of each thing.

Just slightly breathless she speaks to me
of different states, the value and power
of mind-body yoga and mind-altering substances,
how flowers and even ordinary plants
seem surrounded in auras of deepest color,

how peace and serenity are contained
within the most oblique shades of feeling.
Turning back from the line of her conversation,
looking down into the peaches sinking
beneath the white cream, I see each of them

framed within the gold necklace stitched
at the edge of the cobalt blue bowl. I hear
the blend of other voices close from many
into one and open back again, and I wake
to understand this also is an altered state

as when I might round a grey wintry corner
to see the chestnut vendor roasting shells
over a blaze of wood chips which consume
themselves and rise up seamless as smoke
into the mist of evening, each one seeming

to fall without weight from the furthest depth
of galactic space as he lets them drop, one
by one, into the bag. Or, seeing more slowly,
seeing as a window into the mind, as when
I turn through the dark book of Velasquez, see

shadow upon shade the young face of Phillipe
Prospero who was not so much imbecilic
as sensitive and living in sadness, the whole
of his life, it must have seemed to him,
enclosed within the harsh rasp of chairs

echoing across oaken floors where the sounds
of amorous court laughter entered unasked
into his ears. They fastened silver bells
to his long, priest-like, linen cassock,
in the hope he might hear only the intricate

linking of their melodic chimes. It was
a state so real he seemed to live more of life
than he could bear, in but a few years.
Is there, then, any moment which is not
so distinct as to seem as if it were lit

by the sun of a different season, as I breathe
or do not, read this page or not, step, eat,
perceive, or not, full in this shifting blaze
of consciousness where I go on reaching out
to seek myself again, anew, able to be renewed.

GRIEF IN THE AMERICAN GRAIN

The year was 1968, my brother began to smoke
marijuana. The colors in the sky were violet
when he played. The saxophonist invited him
to go further. Ten years later he lay
in a wordless coma. At that same moment

my son saw his mind so enlarged
by chemical light there was nothing left in him
but tangled streams of language turning
into frames of fantasy. For what now seems
longer than years my daughter's abundant

woman energy has been driven by powder
from the coca plant. She cannot eat or sleep.
She cannot wake to the ordinary light
of ordinary day. Now it is 1990,
I am east of New York, far off from those

I once loved, a small boat going faster
than I would have chosen, down a great river —
this river which we think of as the stream of time
but which slowly I have come to understand
is the unmarked river of being, bearing

each of us equally, each separately, in a way
that reflects the way we see ourselves in it.
Grief has not left, my friend says, and now
I understand that behind these not yet
accepted memories, mine has not. Day after day

I walk beneath the branches of trees, moving
in and out of sunlight. The sun releases
the threads of its energy to me. Salt sweat
comes forth and flows. Don't wear your sadness
pinned to your coat, my quiet conscience says,

there are others who will receive. I feel myself
as that person and that person, each who receives.
Sadness passes through me, begins to pass on.
I force my legs forward. Sweat goes on rising
from within a network of veins I cannot see.

There is nothing ill in the world, I know,
but my own thought, clouded by loss, drifting
in chambered cells, drinking dark blood,
walking with my brother, walking with my children,
trying to find the current of my own search.

AUTUMN MORNING

My eyes shift from the mirror. Its legs
are shaped like the letter *n* where
they lower themselves, meet the floor.
It has a large body and an orange, speckled
underbody which I think I remember
belongs to the female tarantula. I raise

then lower my shoe. Its legs and frame
give a snap and sharp crunching as if
the vowels and consonants of a word have been
forced together, make a packet so dense
it is equal to the life which all at once
they are giving up. What do I understand,

standing with white soap surrounding
my nose and eyes? It is still necessary
to take up the razor. I am still asking
this local, hourly universe which feels
effortless in its forms and composed of every
sort of creature, to forgive, to comprehend.

Large voices and large, many-tiered claims
have grown into my life with such a constant,
advancing hunger they feel like vines
which edge out in fingers to take over
the panes of a window. Claims have taken
my arms and mind, I can no longer imagine

I have the time to gather it into a box,
move it out to the bushes behind the house.
It is clear I have nodded at death
from the height of human clock time
and walked on past, assumed the next moment
would turn open, reveal from within

the eye of its breath, a state of being
which I might believe forgave me, as if
I were alive in a part of the world
where life could migrate at any instant,
has no fear of death, sees itself printed
in the face of death, can step forward,

speak unaltered the harsh and muddy
clash of change. I hear no voice, I sense
no rustling of curtains being parted
to mark a place of acceptance and benediction.
In the presence of my own presence, I see
I am living without awareness of even

my own foot, each of whose bones is curling
inward, trying to free itself from the clotted
strands of shell and membrane still
clinging to them and swinging slowly about
like sticks of broken, lost furniture.

BLOOD AND BLOOD RED

It was not the dark, clotted,
reddish-brown I remembered. It was
a bright, glowing red which spoke
without hesitation — I am clear,

I carry the light of the skies
through the veins of the body.
I shine with the intensity of one
who lives alone but is not alone,

who runs as a stream past the islands
of the heart, the spleen, washes
and is washed by them. I carry energy
of rice and energy of beans, the white

hearts of almonds and of artichokes,
I carry the waste left after.
I carry waste and I am not diminished.
Across sloping plains of muscle

I move with the sliding grace of rivers.
In the mountain valleys of the brain
my veins are as thin as a spider's
finely spun web. I live in timeless

darkness, but announce the living eye
of light when skin is cut and I flow out.
I announce forests and rivers of person,
age standing to sing and youth sighing,

I announce the bright ocean of organs
in the coat of that color which long ago
some mat-haired Saxon, standing
and looking upon a wounded bison,

spoke with the sound which was the sound red.

At a Crossroads Beyond the City

Standing at the crossroads of yes-but,
an Arab-Indian woman came toward me.
What she brought, I later understood,
was the light covering the face of her

timeless self. With her life and my own
we sat in the hands of feeling,
the trees spread their limbs over us,
the sky gave up its ideas like rain.

She lent her eyes with the openness of sunrise
directly to me. The edges of ourselves,
she slowly said, form the shapes of our cage.
The trees came fully into leaf.

The sky went on loosing its rain.

You/I

You understood. I understood.
When my hand came close to the earth
of your flesh, there was as much, no,
more energy connecting us as when

it touched. I passed this palm,
the ends of these fingers, down one arm —
your darkness took me in. Down one leg —
my lightness lifted you. It was then

almost evening, there was further to go.
We saw we could begin at any moment.
Further, later, early morning we went in.
Further longer later we went on in.

And if later still we part, I will eat
my lungs my heart from the inside out,
a man separated from his substance,
though seeming to walk everywhere about.

THROUGH WHICH DOOR

Through which door was it that you came?
In the beginning I was not there waiting,
and I cannot now remember my own coming in
either. I remember only that I was

already standing in this continuing moment
we have named the present. It was morning,
everything seemed about to lift, fill its lungs,
breathe toward transparency. Walking to that place

in my room which waited as light, and which
when I was older I understood as window,
I could see a tree lay on the ground.
Its leaves seen then from above were very green

where the sun bent its waves in around them.
Many branches lay broken. I went out
with lengths of twine to tie the fractured
sections together. Spring, and a slow, sprawling

rain of birds, small insects, flowering blossoms,
took the fingers of my hand, led them through
the dew-flecked grass. They found branches
they believed they could cure, felt this life

as free, a place where each divided thing
might join. My brother came to the door.
His face was sad, as if it had been dipped
in too much understanding. He had woken alone.

He could not recall which house, which life,
he was standing in. He watched for a time,
his face becoming peaceful, then went back in.
Sometime or years later you could not remember

how you had come in either, or even
that I had held you. You were sad, I went
out in my imagination, turned the voice
of your pain toward the place of forgetting,

came back in. That, it seemed, was the way
of the first door, open if you could see it,
closed if you could not. I stepped close.
I looked in your eyes. I lent you the water-

fall of your own laughter, which had been
waiting throughout your life to explode
the mind's river bed of sadness, where it lay
like a bottomless depth of piled stones.

TOWARD THE END OF THIS CENTURY

Beyond, in Empire rooms, their voices move.
I sit down. In the place of silence I write:
passion I have sung, the ribbed vault of feeling
woven between eyes and the many parts of sense
which link people, anger I have not, yet anger
I have known, alive and speaking in my hands
like a virus loose in the body's system.

I look down the hallway of rooms.
I see the mind and body union of the Greeks
brought forward into painting that it might
enhance the state, dignify Presidents, while
countless others of us sleep under bridges
and search after beer cans with plastic
garbage bags. All of this I would leave

and go away from. Anger, I understand,
was rage at the day-by-day positioning of each
against the other. Cocktails and the Cup Hunt.
The smiles of diplomats glowing in the eyes
of butter knives. I stop. I rise. It is night.
It is spring. Walking, I drift out past
box hedges standing motionless on the terrace,

past stables and an empty pavilion, down
to an arbor and the dream-like movement
of flowing water. Leaves and now a white-winged
egret are floating past. Where does he go?
I no longer think I care. And yet. And yet
from behind each thought and from within
every sadness, from the immeasurable distance

of a tribal hunter's past, I see that I do care.
I see he is breath-empowered like us and freely
moving in this larger stream of mountains
and rivers, forests and seas, all the faces
of consciousness which we think of as life
and which spread out like a robe around us
to include the dark, bone-bare, window of death.

I nod and wish him well, I wish him clear,
continuing water. I send whatever I have of care,
of concern one for the other, which we call love.
I send them all love, each their own measure,
where they stand, nod together, talk on. I turn
and cross on. Slowly I raise my arms. It is dawn.
It is spring. I can see that we are young still.

After Reading Izumi Shikibu's Haiku

At 50th Street the door at the end of the car opened
without anyone being there. Shikibu's haiku
stood before me. "While watching the long rains
falling on this world my heart too, fades
with the unseen color of the spring flowers."

Understand, remember, I was saying to myself,
you cannot be freed from the forking limbs
of this life's longings simply with discipline,
you will need to hold each of them up like dreams
before the sun, let the wind of far-distant light

pass through. I could see the unhindered
eye of the translator, a woman with a face
as luminous as the waters of a still pond,
freely transcribing Shikibu's calligraphs
in this city where dollar signs are continually

being tied to the mind of each thing.
She had entered the calm at rest behind desire
which filled the heart of that courtesan. Shikibu
had lived through the doubled-up fist of war
which shatters each thing, and the passionate eyes

of lovers which enhance each. She had lived
through the dark earth of her daughter's death
and through her husband's, and had arrived
at a mountain monastery where each moment
was felt as open, in movement, a continuous

offering from which one might receive all things.
Now they were joined, the translator from the new
civilization of certitude, and the courtesan
wearing every face of change. I looked up
to look away, to let thought pass away,

saw him step from a darkness between the cars
as deep as if it were the not yet imagined face
of a second universe. He began to sing of Jesus
and his timeless love. His voice came forth
to form a layered flower of fullness, a rich

voice rising from a slight body which itself
was colored the red-brown of Arkansas River mud
where it flows south out of my remembering.
Coins rose and fell in his cup. The clink
of metal striking metal joined the muffled

sliding of his crutch, mingled with the rustling
of Shikibu's bed clothes, the blinking
eyes of passengers shifting and looking away
from anything which might look back at them.
So many strands drawn into one moment,

I could not hold them. He went on up the car,
the back of his knee was colored a deep,
purple-blue and swollen as large as his thigh.
I could not understand, could not explain,
and even as I write, each thing surrounding him

feels worn down, misshapen. And if I were to step
from this train, walk the corners of this city,
I could not comprehend the depth of his suffering,
the sense of his being entirely alone. I stood.
I drew coins from my pocket, put them back.

I moved forward, I would try to speak with him,
I would seek to find words as felt, as direct,
as the lines of a newly-etched calligraph.

ABOUT THE AUTHOR

WILLIAM KISTLER was president of Poets and
Writers for five years. He was also a founding
member and is currently treasurer of Poet's House.
He is the author of two volumes of poetry: *The
Elizabeth Sequence,* which won the Oklahoma Book
Award in 1989, and *America February* (1991). In
1992 he co-edited and wrote the lead essay for
Buying America Back, a collection of essays on
America's social and economic problems.